Original title:
Succulent Secrets

Author: Derek Caldwell
ISBN HARDBACK: 978-1-80581-904-2
ISBN PAPERBACK: 978-1-80581-431-3
ISBN EBOOK: 978-1-80581-904-2

Veiled Treasures in Arid Soils

In gardens where the cacti grin,
Beneath the sun, they hide within.
Little globes of juicy cheer,
With prickly hugs that draw you near.

A treasure map of colors bright,
Those sneaky gems put up a fight.
Dig carefully; they're sly and smart,
These crunchy munchies steal the heart.

The Lure of Hidden Hydration

In pots so small, the wonders dwell,
With juicy bursts that cast a spell.
A sip of green, they tease and play,
In parched terrain, they rule the day.

A secret stash of thirsty glee,
With petals wide as eyes can see.
Hydration hides in forms so bold,
These secret sweets, their tales unfold.

Soft Radiance in Sun-Kissed Shadows

In twilight glow, they blush and beam,
With plumpness that we all can dream.
A wink of color, soft and shy,
They chuckle softly as we sigh.

In playful pots, they boast their charms,
With cozy curves that welcome arms.
In dusky hues, their laughter sings,
These little treats with joyful flings.

Morsels of Green Beneath Multi-Hued Skies

Beneath a sky of swirling hues,
Lie treasures dressed in bright, bold views.
Each little bite a work of art,
With cheeky grins that warm the heart.

They dance and sway, a lively crew,
As breezes tickle, they bid adieu.
In every leaf, a hidden jest,
These crispy bits are truly blessed.

The Alchemy of Sun and Soil

In a pot of laughter, green things sprout,
The sun tickles leaves, they wiggle about.
A dash of dirt, a sprinkle of cheer,
Who knew plants could make us roar with jeer?

Digging in gardens, we wear silly hats,
Talking to cacti, and petting the chats.
The earth whispers secrets, we giggle in glee,
As flowers tell tales, as wild as can be.

Enigmatic Beauty in Spiny Existence

A spiky affair, the prickliest show,
Each thorny embrace, an awkward hello.
Yet hidden within, a soft, tender heart,
Who knew that this prick would play such a part?

With laughter we dance, avoiding the sting,
Admiring the art that the weird plants bring.
We jest with the jades, in shades of delight,
In nature's own comedy, the humor feels right.

Sweet Succor of the Searing Sands

In deserts so dry, where the heat makes you sweat,
The plants throw a party, and you're their pet.
With shades of green, like a whimsical dream,
They cheer through the drought, a ridiculous theme.

A sip of cool water, like treasure, they keep,
Mirthful in sunlight, where others would weep.
They're sipping on rays, with a giggle and grin,
The desert's own secret, a party within.

Ancient Wisdom in Fleshy Forms

Fleshy and funny, they wobble and jive,
With wisdom so deep, they seem very alive.
They listen with patience, these chubby old souls,
Bouncing through life, in their plump, funny roles.

Tales of the ages, in colors so bright,
They glow in the dark, a peculiar sight.
Their laughter erupts, when the sun starts to set,
A world full of jest, that we won't soon forget.

Unveiling Hidden Blooms

In the pot behind the door,
A cactus wears a floral crown.
It whispers, 'I was once décor,
Now I'm the talk of the town.'

A succulent's got quite the plot,
It sways as if it's in a dance.
With leaves that twist, it's got the shot,
To steal your heart at just a glance.

Dancing Shadows of Green

In the garden, a playful breeze,
The aloe waves, a friendly tease.
It sways in rhythm, oh what a sight,
While sipping sunlight, feeling bright.

Glimpses of joy, the flora knows,
Each tiny leaf, a story grows.
So when you stop and take a peek,
Prepare for laughter, tunes unique!

Cradles of Survival

There’s a plant that surely grins,
With roots so deep, it's where it begins.
It laughs at drought, a true delight,
Adventures hiding, out of sight.

Tiny pots, big personalities,
Living life with such anomalies.
Gardening mischief in every nook,
Who knew you'd own a quirky book?

The Flourishing Few

In the corner, one plant's a star,
It winks and giggles from afar.
With glossy leaves, it loves to brag,
While others droop, it gives a wag.

The blooms combine for nature's cheer,
A blooming party, come draw near!
They plot and scheme with such good cheer,
Who knew these greens would commandeer?

The Enigma of Edible Succulents

Green squish on my plate,
Are you food or a plant?
I give you a taste,
And watch my friends chant.

With thoughts of cuisine,
Who knew cacti could munch?
They giggle and lean,
As they savor the crunch.

A prickly affair,
In salads, you shine bright!
But don't be too bare,
Or you’ll give quite a fright!

So here’s to the greens,
That often perplex us,
They burst at the seams,
With flavor, no fuss!

Serpentine Stems and Starlit Skies

In gardens at night,
Those stems start to sway,
Dancing with delight,
In a silly ballet.

The moon gives a wink,
While I munch with a grin,
I can’t help but think,
Are they laughing within?

Those spiky delights,
With shadows they play,
Under twinkling lights,
They lead me astray.

A serpent of green,
In pajamas I feast,
What state have I seen?
Is it dream or a beast?

Tucked Away in Nature's Hand

Tucked under a rock,
A treasure I find,
With a quirky clock,
That ticks in my mind.

Who knew earth could smile,
With leaves full of cheer?
I'll stay for a while,
With my buddies right here.

A shady retreat,
Where secrets unfold,
With flavors so sweet,
And laughter untold.

I nibble and giggle,
As friends join the spree,
Nature, she wiggles,
Come share this with me!

Silent Guardians of the Gulch

Quietly they stand,
In a rocky domain,
With legs made of sand,
And no need of a brain.

They guard all the snacks,
With spines oh so bold,
One blink and who acts?
The stories they hold!

In the back of my mind,
They plot and they scheme,
With flavors entwined,
They dance in my dream.

So here's to the bunch,
With a wink and a sigh,
I'll share them for lunch,
So come laugh and try!

Hidden Gems in Arid Gardens

In gardens dry, where cacti smile,
Hiding treasures in little while.
Beneath spines sharp, a dance so sly,
They wink at passers, oh me, oh my!

A lizard laughs, in shadows hid,
As plants discuss their playful bid.
Who’ll bloom first, in colors bright?
Wagering under the moonlight!

Underneath the Velvet Soil

Beneath the earth, they have a ball,
Tiny roots throw a wiggly haul.
Dirt's a party, no need for flair,
With worms and bugs, they share a chair!

The cactus jokes in prickly tones,
While snails hum tunes, in hushed undertones.
“What's the hurry?” a wise sage asks,
“Life’s a slow drink, no need for masks!”

Sips of Life in Drought

A droplet's worth a thousand jokes,
As thirsty plants play poker strokes.
"Your turn to bluff!" the aloes cheer,
While agaves sip their cactus beer!

In dry spells, laughter fills the air,
As each new sprout dons a jaunty hair.
The sun's a bully, but they outshine,
With quips and quirks, they intertwine!

Echoes of Ancient Succulents

Old ones whisper tales of yore,
Of potting woes and garden lore.
They chuckle softly in the breeze,
As roots entwine like old-time pleas.

“Water’s overrated,” they snicker low,
“Let the sun do its fiery show!
Who needs a drink when you’re this bold?
We thrive on laughter, not just gold!”

Oasis of Silent Growth

In the corner, plants conspire,
With whispers of thirst and fire.
They giggle as raindrops tease,
'The sun's too bright, we need a breeze!'

Potting soil's their favorite bed,
With dreams of flowers in their head.
Yet when the water starts to flow,
They splatter dirt in a messy show!

Dancers in the Dry Wind

Cacti sway in desert swagger,
As tumbleweeds laugh and stagger.
The sun spins tales of blazing fun,
While lizards dance and bask in sun.

A prickly crew, they joke in waves,
In sandy skirts, they feel like braves.
'Look at us,' the spines declare,
'We're the stars without a care!'

Tales from Tenacious Terrains

Amidst the rocks, the flowers bloom,
Defying odds in nature's room.
With humor sharp like thorns can be,
They jest about their chemistry.

'Who needs water?' the succulents say,
'We're thriving here, come join the play!'
In dust and grit, they find their charm,
They bask in sun without alarm.

Petals of Purity

In a garden where secrets lie,
Petals giggle as breezes sigh.
The bees all buzz, with mischief planned,
While butterflies flit, so unplanned.

'No drama here, just pollen games,'
They chant in floral, silly names.
With colors bright, they put on shows,
In nature's world, anything goes!

Luminescent Resilience in Dry Havens

In the dust, they strut with flair,
Green coats shining, quite the pair.
They sip from raindrops—what a treat!
Dancing shadows with tiny feet.

Laughter blooms among the cacti,
Who knew they'd be so snazzy?
With prickly jokes and playful puns,
They shine like stars, just having fun!

The sand may try to dry them out,
But they waltz in drought without a doubt.
With roots like soldiers, standing proud,
In the heat, they sing out loud!

So let the sun blaze overhead,
These little champs won't fill with dread.
For resilience wears the best of hats,
In dry havens, even the funnies pratt!

Vibrant Unravelings of Hidden Flora.

In corners where the sunlight lingers,
Sprout tiny hands with wiggly fingers.
They giggle softly, wave, and tease,
In hues so bright, they aim to please.

What's this? A bloom with a glow?
I'd wear it if it didn't grow!
They may be small, but oh, so bold,
They've secrets that they never told.

From pots to plots, they jump about,
Shouting, "Hey, look at me, no doubt!"
With wavy tails that brush the ground,
Their shenanigans are quite renowned.

Who knew that greens could catch the eye?
With quirks that always make you sigh.
These vibrant tales of fun and play,
In hidden realms, they rule the day!

Whispers of Waxy Leaves

Hushed tones of nature, soft and sly,
Waxy leaves winking, oh my, oh my!
"Come closer," they whisper, "don't be shy,
We know a joke that'll make you cry!"

With glistening coats and a shiny sheen,
They tell of summers where they've been.
Through desert winds and sizzling rays,
Their laughter echoes on lazy days.

"Did you hear about the thirsty ground?
It slipped on water and fell down!"
These leaves delight in playful words,
Rehearsing jokes with fluttering birds.

So if you wander where they creep,
Prepare for tales, both wild and deep.
For in this realm of waxy glee,
The fun unfolds, just wait and see!

Hidden Nectar of the Desert

In the parched expanse where few things sip,
Nectar flows from nature's quirked lip.
“Come taste our sweetness,” they slyly say,
“To laughter and joy, come join the play!”

Little critters parade in line,
“Here’s a taste, oh how divine!”
With sticky tongues and silly face,
They dive right into this sweet embrace.

A bloom spills joy like candy rain,
In this desert land, there's no disdain.
They giggle, they wiggle, with nectar pure,
In sweet confections, we find the cure.

So raise a glass to the hidden treats,
Where every sip brings crazy feats.
In secret buds and floral cheer,
The nectar’s calling, come draw near!

Taming the Desolate

In a garden of cacti, I found my muse,
Dancing with spines, I'd rather not bruise.
Each poke is a lesson, a point of delight,
Nature’s own humor, it’s quite a sight.

With pots full of petals, I amused my fate,
Who knew thorny companions could turn out so great?
I laughed at the weeds as they tried to invade,
Their plans were derailed, oh what a charade!

So here in my haven, I spread joy and glee,
Just me and my plants, as wild as can be.
With soil on my hands and thoughts all awry,
I twirl with the daisies, let worries fly high.

Now teaching the ferns how to salsa and sway,
They’re learning my rhythm, come join in the play!
In a patch of odd blooms, we all share a grin,
Who knew being green could cause such a spin?

Unforeseen Blooms

In a corner forgotten, a flower did sprout,
With petals so tiny, it stood up and bowed.
"Didn't see me coming?" it shouted with glee,
Surprising the flowers as bold as can be.

A cactus in bloom held a confetti parade,
Dressed up for the party, in sunlight it played.
With neighbors so jealous, it giggled aloud,
"Know your spines, dear friends, they're what make you proud!"

An orchid went sneaky, with colors so bright,
It wiggled and jiggled, oh what a sight!
"Look at me, world, I'm a star in disguise,
Who knew blooms could twirl and cause such surprise?"

So here in the wild where odd things convene,
Each petal and leaf wears their quirkiest sheen.
With laughter in gardens, we'll flourish and sing,
Together we blossom, what wonders we bring!

Vignettes of Charming Resilience

There once was a sprout with a heart full of dreams,
Beneath the old fence, it plotted and schemed.
With sunlight the fuel and rain as its cheer,
It stretched for the stars, refusing all fear.

A wild little weed broke out into song,
"Hey, look at me, I've been here all along!"
With dandelion wishes on wind's gentle breath,
It laughed at the lawn mow, defying its death.

Amongst all the glass, a brave little leaf,
Said, "I'll show you how to embrace disbelief!"
It danced in the breeze, oh so sprightly and clear,
Finding joy in the chaos, it offered a cheer.

In gardens of laughter, where plants play their role,
We find in each other a mutual goal.
To bloom in the moments, both silly and bright,
In the tapestry of life, we're a shared delight!

The Guardian of Hidden Hydration

In the garden where the cacti play,
A spiky knight guards his juicy sway.
With laughter bubbling up from every thorn,
He whispers secrets of hydration, reborn.

He dons a crown made of plump green leaves,
Chasing away the thirsty and naive.
His trusty sidekick, a sly little bug,
Finds shady spots for the hydration hug.

When rain does fall, they jump with glee,
Dancing in puddles like a wild spree.
But watch your step, or you'll slip and slide,
On the slick ode to nature's slippery side!

So raise a glass, dear friends of zest,
To the guardian who knows hydration best.
With every sip, raise up a cheer,
For the knight in the garden, that water dear!

Marvels of Nature's Hand

In gardens where the oddities sprout,
Little wonders dance about.
A cactus with a goofy grin,
Boasts stories of the sun within.

The octopus plant sways with flair,
Tickling the breeze without a care.
They gossip joyfully, oh so grand,
Of magic made by nature's hand.

Each bloated bloom a jester's face,
Sprinkling humor, the leafy grace.
With roots that wriggle in prancing glee,
They juggle rain like a jubilee.

So come, dear pals, lend an ear,
To nature’s jesters, bring good cheer.
In every leaf and stem, you'll find,
A chuckle waiting—purely designed!

A Symphony of Juicy Stories

In the realm where the fruits collide,
A symphony of tales, juicy and wide.
With banter and beats of the garden floor,
Every berry bobs, eager for more.

A pineapple sang with a flourish so bright,
While the oranges rolled, chuckling in delight.
The mangoes danced, their sweetness profound,
Transforming the breeze into a fun sound!

Beneath the sun, stories intertwine,
The nectar flows, making all align.
Oh, the rhythm of vines in a quirky tune,
Bouncing along with the giggling moon.

So raise a fruit, let laughter ring,
Join the chorus of nature's swing.
In every bite and every cheer,
Lies a juicy story, oh so dear!

The Life Within the Thorn

Beneath the thorn, a laugh does bloom,
As prickly pals huddle in cozy room.
With tiny spiders weaving tales of glee,
And laughter bubbling up like a tea!

A ladybug winks from her leafy throne,
Sipping nectar with a funny bone.
In this sharp abode, life is a tease,
As cacti chortle in the soft breeze.

Each prick a punchline, crazy and quick,
In the garden where surprises click.
So tread with humor, go easy on the feet,
For the life within, is a humorous feat!

Gather 'round, let your spirits soar,
For in each thorn, there’s always more.
With giggles and gasps, let’s uncork the fun,
In the life within these thorns, we run!

The Grace of Resurgence in Fragile Bodies

In gardens where the sunbeams play,
A wilting plant had much to say.
"I thought I'd met my twilight time,
But look! I'm back, and life is prime!"

With roots that danced in joyous glee,
They swayed like sprites, wild and free.
"A sip of rain, some rays of light,
And here I am, a lovely sight!"

The neighbors stared, quite dumbfounded,
As leaves returned, green and unbounded.
"Was that a miracle?" they mused,
Or merely luck that they had used?

So let it be, the jest we weave,
Fragile lives that won't decease.
With a chuckle, we toast the thrill,
Of nature's knack to bend and heal.

Soft Surprises in Nature's Drought

In a landscape dry as a crunchy chip,
A little sprout made a daring trip.
"I've got the knack for finding drinks,
While others worry, I just think!"

The sun was blazing, the ground was pale,
Yet this brave bud began to sail.
"Fetch me a cloud! I'll tease the sky,
And watch the drought go woefully by!"

A dance of roots beneath the bluff,
Brought up a sip; oh, wasn't that tough!
"To bravely bloom amid such thirst,
Is nothing short of love - and cursed!"

So laughter echoed, and cheers went high,
A celebration beneath the spine.
For nothing dulls a feisty cheer,
In nature's tide, we persevere!

Tales Told by Thorny Companions

Two prickly pals stared down the lane,
With twisted jokes and knowing grins.
"Why do we poke?" one asked with glee,
"To keep the curious far from me!"

Their thorns were sharp, their humor slick,
Gossiping all about the prick!
"I once knew a rose who lost a petal,
Now she's a star in a flower battle!"

"And what about the cactus up the hill?
He started dancing and gave us a thrill!
He wore a hat made of old twine,
And claimed sunburn wasn't a crime!"

So laughter rolled through the sunlit space,
As thorny friends shared jokes with grace.
Come join their tale, no need to fret,
In spiky times, there's fun, you bet!

Elixirs of Life in Verdant Terraces

Amidst the rows of emerald hues,
A bloom concocted wondrous brews.
"A splash of sun and a drizzle of dew,
And watch what magic I can do!"

With giggles, leaves began to sway,
As herbs mixed up a savory play.
"A pinch of happiness, maybe a dash,
And soon we'll have quite the splash!"

"Last week, I found an old recipe,
From wise old roots, come dance with me!
For drops of joy bestow great cheer,
When sprinkled mild, we hold them dear!"

So on their terraces, good vibes brewed,
The plants were smiling, uproar ensued.
Life's elixirs, stirred with delight,
In nature's kitchen, all felt right!

Secrets Buried in Blushing Blooms

In gardens lush, with colors bright,
Are tales hidden, quite a sight.
The daisies giggle, the roses wink,
While tulips plot over some drink.

With every petal, a chuckle lies,
The garden's gossip, oh what a surprise!
Each bloom knows of the bees' great dance,
And how they woo with floral romance.

But watch the violets—they're quite sly,
They hold secrets they never supply.
When the sun sets, they spin their tales,
Of adventures with frogs and snail trails.

So tiptoe softly, don't break the spell,
For blooms might laugh louder than you can tell.
In vibrant hues, their laughs take flight,
Buried secrets in blushing delight.

The Whispering Breath of Drought Survivors

In the dry heat, a cactus grins,
With spiky arms, it throws the wins.
It sips on whispers from the breeze,
And chuckles softly amidst the trees.

"Water, water, what a fuss!"
It smirks at those who ride the bus.
While others wilt in scorching sun,
This spiny hero has all the fun.

A laughing lizard scuttles by,
With tales of raindrops from the sky.
"Did you see the drip?" it slyly sneers,
"Such drama in our drought-filled years!"

So heed the laughter in the dry,
These warriors bloom, they twist and try.
With every breath, a joke unfolds,
In desert tales secretly told.

Mysteries Wrapped in Petal and Pith

The garden's a puzzle, quite the tease,
Wrapped in petals that rustle in the breeze.
Roses hide whispers, daisies hold sighs,
Beneath the bright look, a scheme surely lies.

With every bloom comes a little jest,
Where purple pansies throw a wild fest.
They dance and twirl, giggling loud,
While sunflowers nod, oh so proud.

“Did you hear the one about the bee?”
It buzzed around, so full of glee.
While nectar dreams fill shadows at night,
Petals confide in the moonlight bright.

So gather near and listen close,
To flowers who tease, we love them most.
In the blooming riddle, let laughter unfurl,
In mysteries wrapped, life’s a swirl.

Blossoms of Resilience in Parched Realms

In lands where water takes a break,
Blooms pop up, oh for heaven's sake!
With roots that hold through thick and thin,
They smile at drought, ready to win.

"Look at us thrive!" the sunflowers boast,
"With courage like ours, we need a toast!"
While shadows play on a sun-baked stone,
They dance in dirt, claiming their throne.

Laughter erupts from a creased old leaf,
Holding secrets, refusing grief.
With every drop—a story to share,
In parched realms, they flourish with flair.

So tip your hat to blooms so spry,
In arid lands, they reach for the sky.
With smiles so bright in desert light,
They remind us to relish every bite!

Nature's Quiet Conspiracies

In the garden, whispers grow,
Plants plot, but they don’t show.
With roots entwined like old friends,
Their laughter's where the mischief ends.

A tulip tells a rose a tale,
Of ants who dance and snails who sail.
They chat beneath the sunlit beams,
About the hearts and crazy dreams.

Some daisies wear their petals tight,
Throwing shade in morning light.
While ferns with frowns conspire deep,
To keep their secrets locked in sleep.

Oh, what a ruckus they can make,
With every rustle, giggle, quake.
In gardens where the wild things roam,
Nature's jokes feel just like home.

Cacti Chronicles

In a desert filled with prickly pride,
Cacti giggle, they cannot hide.
Their spikes are sharp but hearts are soft,
Making jokes of windblown wafts.

One bold soul tried to wear a hat,
But ended up just looking flat.
With arms held high, they start to dance,
While tumbleweeds roll by in chance.

There’s laughter when a cholla sneezes,
Sending prickles in the breezes.
Hilarious tales of pot and soil,
Under the sun, they calmly toil.

In a sandy realm of joy and jest,
Each cactus aims to be the best.
While others take the crown so fast,
These pricky pals will simply last.

Enigmatic Greens of the Earth

Amidst the greens, a riddle grows,
With glee it sprouts, where nobody knows.
The leaves have secrets, deep and bright,
With laughter echoing in the night.

A wandering vine sings to the trees,
While ferns sway softly in the breeze.
The playful moss has tales to tell,
Of crazy critters and where they dwell.

In shadows thick, the jokes will bloom,
From croaking frogs that clear the room.
A handsome sprout with style, no doubt,
Sways to tunes no one talks about.

Oh, dancing greens and giggling leaves,
Crafting humor in nature's weaves.
In every twist, there's mirth to see,
In these green realms, happy as can be.

Inner World of Plump Leaves

In a world where leaves are round,
Laughter swells without a sound.
With every plump and jolly quirk,
They plot their jokes while others work.

A leaf named Larry tells a lie,
That raindrops live to learn to fly.
While others whisper, ‘Did you hear?’
Of dew drops knitting cozy gear.

Those plump greens laugh at sun's warm grin,
While counting ants that stumble in.
They trade their tales in secret nooks,
In the pages of their leafy books.

Inside this world of colors bright,
Every leaf hides pure delight.
In nature's tale, the smiles abound,
In the plumpest leaves, our fun is found.

Woven Wonders of the Arid

In deserts bright, they pop up high,
With colors bold that catch the eye.
Some wear a hat, some sport a dress,
Who knew plants could make such a mess?

They sip on sun, they dine on dew,
A cactus party, just a few.
In crackled earth, they spread their cheer,
With tiny quirks that bring a sneer.

Ribbed and round, or tall and spry,
They laugh at rain, just wave goodbye.
In prickled coats, they strut their stuff,
Sassy little gremlins, aren't they tough?

So here's to those who thrive in sand,
With spiky hugs, their clever plans.
In every twist, a laughter rings,
Oh, how they flaunt their wacky things!

Parables in Prickly Pairs

Two cactus stand, their arms out wide,
Challenging folks to take a ride.
With prickly pears that taste so sweet,
A culinary risky treat!

They tell a tale of thirsty nights,
Of scaredy bugs and silly fights.
With every poke, a giggle bursts,
Who knew plants could quench such thirsts?

Amongst the thorns, they plot and scheme,
A juicy fruit, a dreamer's dream.
With laughter echoing through the grove,
They share their tales of spiky love.

So pluck a pear, and let it shine,
With every bite, joy intertwines.
Funny friends in nature's jest,
The prickly pals, they are the best!

Beauty Behind the Spikes

With every spike, a tale untold,
A world of beauty, brave and bold.
They wear their armor, stand so proud,
Yet shine in sunlight, draw a crowd.

Petals peeking through the thorns,
In playful dances, beauty adorns.
Each twist and turn, a wink, a nod,
Making the desert seem less odd.

Their colors pop in bright display,
As curious critters come to play.
In nature's art, there lies a spark,
Of laughter shared in the dark.

So don’t you frown, embrace the fun,
With spiky friends, the joy’s begun.
A world of wonder waits in sight,
Behind the spikes, there lies delight!

Whispered Myths of Bulbous Beauty

Gather 'round for tales so grand,
Of bulbous wonders in the sand.
They whisper myths of mirthful days,
In plump little forms, they like to play.

With round, fat cheeks, they tell a joke,
Bouncing about till someone chokes.
In playful puffs, they swell with pride,
A roly-poly plant, they provide!

A twist of fate, a sunny grin,
Filled with juice and laughter within.
Each plump companion, quirky and bright,
Bringing joy, a sheer delight.

So heed the tales of bulbous dreams,
Where laughter flows in sunlit beams.
In every curve, a secret's spun,
In whispered myths, we're all in fun!

Secrets Beneath the Succulents

In a garden where odd things grow,
Cacti whisper truths we don’t know.
A turtle once tried to play hide and seek,
But found spiky friends, oh, what a cheek!

Rabbits hop by with a wink and a grin,
They munch on greens, let the chaos begin!
And those sneaky weeds? They just can’t be tamed,
In their leafy frolic, they’ve boldly proclaimed.

At dusk, when the sun dips low,
Plants gather 'round in a secret show.
Their leaves dance wildly, a botanical jam,
Even the soil’s giggling, oh, what a sham!

So if you tiptoe past this lively scene,
Don’t spill the beans, keep their joy serene.
For the secrets we share beneath the bright moon,
Are merely the laughter of nature’s own tune.

Lush Landscapes of Resilience

In a world where the bold plants grow,
Daisies threw parties filled with cheer and glow.
Sunflowers swayed, all decked out in style,
Flipping to the sun, they did it with a smile!

The bromeliads sang their bubbly song,
"To thrive in this land where we all belong!"
While toads in ponds threw a wild dance,
Inviting the beetles to join in their prance.

Mighty oaks laughed, they're not shy at all,
As squirrels darted up, attempting to sprawl.
"Let's stockpile acorns!" they'd shout with glee,
But droppings and mess just ruined the spree!

Yet through all the antics in foliage vast,
Laughter and joy free-skate unsurpassed.
So gaze at this vibrant and humorous scene,
Nature's a jokester, and it's split at the seam!

The Art of Water Storage

In a drought where plants droop and sigh,
Cacti boast, “Look at us, oh my!”
While other greens fret with disbelief,
These spiny heroes store water like a chief.

A barrel cactus? Oh, what a show!
Sprinkling tales of hydration glow.
“Just a sprinkle here, a splash over there,
We sip like champions, eat your heart out, dear!”

So when thirsty whispers ride the breeze,
Cacti just chuckle, “Oh, please, oh, please!”
They sip from the sun, with each passing ray,
While others panic, feeling the sway.

In the heart of the arid, they dance and twirl,
Crafting drought tales with a leafy swirl.
So tip your hat to these spiky friends,
They’re the jesters of dryness, their fun never ends!

Thorns and Tenderness

In a garden of laughter, what an odd sight,
Thorns and sweetness holding on tight.
Roses giggle as they point to the crew,
Who knew sharpness could be so askew?

A prickly pear stood with a grin ear to ear,
"Compassion is tough, but we're all in here!"
While daisies nod in a fluffy ballet,
Waltzing through prickers, come what may.

"Oh come on, dear friend, just give us a smile,
Despite the sharp edges, we're friends all the while!"
And while cactus and thorns seem rough and unkind,
Inside beats a heart with camaraderie blind.

So next time you stumble on prickles and pains,
Remember the sweetness that often remains.
For in nature's patchwork of laughter and tears,
Thorns can hold tenderness throughout the years!

Secrets of the Spiky Tribe

In a land where prickers reign,
Cacti dance beneath the rain.
They wear their thorns like fancy hats,
And sip on puddles—imagine that!

With a giggle and a poke,
These spiky friends, they often joke.
"We're sharp, but don't fret, it's just our flair!"
They crack up while we comb our hair.

Nectar of the Spines

Oh, the sweetness from the sprout,
Bringing bees and bugs about.
They buzz and hum, the little thieves,
Stirring up our springtime leaves.

With every sip of sugary treat,
The spiny guards feel quite the cheat.
"Protect the juice!" they shimmy and sway,
As candy-loving ants come to play.

The Drought's Embrace

In a dry spell, life's a hoot,
What's a plant to do? Just scoot!
They wiggle roots and stretch up high,
While pigeons look and wonder why.

They whisper tales of rain-soaked dreams,
While sipping sunshine, sipping creams.
"We thrive in grit, we love the squeeze!"
And basking in sun, they giggle with ease.

Curious Growths of Time

Time slows down with every sprout,
Curved and twisted—what's that about?
Some grew wild, some grew tall,
All clearly having a ball!

They share their tales of growth and glee,
Of unexpected heights, oh me, oh my!
With every twist, they wink with cheer,
Singing, "Watch us bloom, we persevere!"

Enchantment Found in Leafy Layers

In the garden where plants gossip,
Poking fun with each leafy twist.
Cacti smile with their prickly jokes,
While daisies roll their eyes, quite miffed.

Underneath the sun's warm glow,
A cabbage wears a jaunty hat.
The tulips giggle, swaying low,
As the roses mutter, 'What's up with that?'

Each green friend boasts a silly tale,
Of snails in race, quite slow and pale.
With whispers shared in soft green hues,
The plants all laugh, they’ve got the cues.

Beneath the moon's enchanting light,
Plants crack puns about the night.
They may be rooted, but oh, what flair!
In this world, laughter's everywhere!

Evocative Echoes of Plant Kinship

In the soil, tales intertwine,
Bromeliads tease with floral chime.
Vines do a jig, tangled but fine,
While succulents sip sun like fine wine.

A fern whispers secrets so bright,
To a sage, who nods with delight.
'You think you're wise?' the basil quips back,
'Try leafing through my herb-filled stack!'

Petunias are plotting their evening spree,
With marigolds grinning, 'Let's dance with glee!'
In this green theater, they're the main act,
Mischief and mirth, that's the plant pact!

Around the pots, laughter erupts,
As witty weeds offer cheeky interrupts.
With petals and prayers, they build their dream,
In a world where plants humorously scheme!

Embracing Life's Tension in Succulent Form

In tight little spaces, they curl up neat,
Squished plants complaining, 'This isn't a treat!'
With succulent sighs, they stretch for the sun,
Though packed like a clown car, they still have fun.

Juggling water, they're experts at play,
Just a drip too much? They gasp, 'No way!'
Their stems all krumping, in photosynthesis style,
These plants keep a rhythm, their roots compile.

The aloe's got humor, a healing refrain,
'Rubbing off on me? Let's share the pain!'
With giggles of gratitude, every leaf does its part,
In life's little circus, they steal your heart.

Flower pots giddy with green camaraderie,
In this garden of wonder, it's laughter we see.
With joy in each layer, they twist and they turn,
In life's leafy comedy, there's always a burn!

Petals Adrift in Wind's Caress

Breezy whispers play with the flowers,
Petals pirouette in carefree hours.
Dancing wildly, they swap their dye,
Swaying as cheeky clouds drift by.

A daisy shouts, 'Catch me if you dare!'
While the sunflowers boast, 'We don't have a care!'
In this ballet of blooms, there's giggling galore,
As petals tumble and flirt with the floor.

The breeze throws shade while everyone spins,
A floral fiesta where laughter begins.
'You're blowing it hard,' the bluebells chime,
But in the sweet chaos, it's all just fine!

With every gust, they rustle their plans,
In this playful waltz, they're all best friends.
So here's to the petals and wind's cheerful jest,
In a world of humor, they find their zest!

Tender Whispers of Verdant Life

Beneath the leaves, a giggle hides,
A cactus cracks jokes, as no one decides.
With every bloom, a snicker appears,
Nature's punchlines, bringing us cheers.

The ferns dance freely, swaying around,
While daisies whisper, oh what a sound!
They share the tales of those who stroll,
In laughter and light, they reach for the goal.

With tiny roots playing peek-a-boo,
They're soft with secrets, but bold with their view.
With petals adorned in colors so bright,
They tickle our senses, a joyous delight.

In gardens so green, the jesters all play,
Where blossoms and greens chase the gloom away.
Each plant has a story, an anecdote sweet,
With laughter embedded in every heartbeat.

Hidden Nectar of the Desert Bloom

Under the sun, the cacti just grin,
With prickly puns that make you spin.
They hide their nectar with clever disguise,
Sweetness awaiting to catch you by surprise.

A sly little flower, so coy and so shy,
Teases the bees as they flutter nearby.
With every sip, they laugh with glee,
No secret's too safe, even in the spree.

The desert watches with a twinkling eye,
As blooms play tricks, oh my, oh my!
Each petal a jest, in sunlight they bask,
In this secret garden, no questions to ask.

When the sun dips low, the jokes take flight,
In shadows and whispers, they share their delight.
With every rustle, a chuckle unfurls,
In the hidden realms of the desert's pearls.

The Silent Language of Green Fingers

In pots and patches, they speak without sound,
With fingers of green, they dance all around.
A wink from the violets, a nudge from the thyme,
Together they giggle, in perfect rhyme.

The herbs plot mischief in soft, sunny spots,
With basil moonwalking and parsley in knots.
The rosemary nods, sharing tales from the past,
While the mint makes a joke that's unsurpassed.

Like whispers of nature, they share silly dreams,
Giggling in sunlight, amidst gentle beams.
Each leaf a riddle, each branch a jest,
In this leafy world, they're always impressed.

Though silent they may be, the fun's never masked,
In colors and forms, they all get unmasked.
Together they flourish, in harmony sing,
A chorus of laughter, as joy they bring.

Lush Hints Beneath Sunlit Skin

Beneath the sunshine, the greens all conspire,
With giggles and wiggles, they're never tired.
The leaves pull pranks, while the roots play coy,
In every little layer, they find boundless joy.

The foliage teases, with just a soft sway,
As if to say, come out and play!
With each fluttering rustle, a joke is spun,
In the tapestry greens, the laughter's begun.

Under the sun, the petals do boast,
With colors so vibrant, they steal every toast.
Each bloom a prankster, so bold and so sweet,
Funny little hints, in their playful retreat.

In the shade of a bough, the whispers convene,
Sharing the tales of the laughter unseen.
A world full of glee, in gardens we roam,
With hints of the funny, it feels just like home.

Shadows of Pleasure in Coastal Terrain

In sandy nooks they giggle, so sly,
Caught in the sun, like doughnuts on high.
They shrink and expand, have rather bold ways,
Whispering secrets in playful sun rays.

Fronds and spines wear a crown of gleam,
A party of greens, or so it would seem.
Their roots do a dance, a silent ballet,
Twirling and swirling, all in joyful play.

Each shapes a grin, in a prickly embrace,
Nature's comedians, a light-hearted chase.
Beneath the broad skies, they jest and they jive,
In shadows of pleasure, oh how they thrive!

So come take a stroll where the fun never ends,
With spiky companions, who need no fake friends.
In coastal terrain where the laughter rings clear,
A garden of giggles, your heart will endear.

The Allure of Botanical Guardians

In pots they conspire, oh such clever sights,
Guardians of plant life, with thorny delights.
They wear capes of green, their humor intact,
Like quirky jesters, they playfully act.

With rich, lavish curves and odd little poses,
They tease out the giggles, like sweet little roses.
Their prickles invite you, but tread with a grin,
A poke full of laughter lies hid deep within.

At gatherings of flora, they tell wild old tales,
Of sunbaked adventures on spiky green trails.
Each leaf a charmer, with stories to share,
In the realm of green laughter, there's love in the air.

So toast to the guardians, with glasses held high,
May they tickle our fancies as days pass us by!
For in their green laughter, a treasure we find,
A garden of humor, oh so intertwined.

Flourishing in the Embrace of Dryness

In sun-scorched realms, they revel and sway,
Wearing hats of dust, in a whimsical way.
With roots deep below, they sip on a joke,
Thirsty for laughs, like sponges they soak.

A cactus performs, in its ribbed, dapper coat,
Telling wild tales with a prickly note.
In parched company, they brightly parade,
Who knew dryness could make such a charade?

Mirth springs from earth, as they learn to adapt,
With humor their armor, they warp and they clap.
In a world full of giggles, they flourish with pride,
Sipping on sunshine, they take it in stride.

So raise up your glasses to those who survive,
In the heat of the moment, they wittily thrive.
With laughter as water, their spirits are clear,
Flourishing brightly, they're the life of the year.

The Quiet Power of Thirsty Hearts

In silence, they whisper, each thirsty heart waits,
With humor and wit, oh the fun that abates.
They drink in the sun, and breathe in the air,
Winking at passers, with their secret affair.

Beneath the dry surface, a party does grow,
A club of oddities, putting on a show.
The smiles that escape from their leathery skins,
An invitation to life, where true laughter begins.

They might look unyielding, with spikes all around,
But charm is their language, breaking all ground.
In their quiet endurance, a jest that won't quit,
Thirsty for joy, but never for wit!

So watch as they flirt with the light through the haze,
In the dance of the drought, they find merry ways.
With hearts wide and thirsty, they flourish so bright,
In laughter's embrace, they sparkle at night.

Blossoms in the Barren

In the desert where cacti dwell,
A tumbleweed told me a tale to sell.
He danced with the wind, oh what a sight,
Wearing a hat made of paper at night.

A flower popped up, quite out of place,
In a sandy patch, it wore a cute face.
It wished for a friend, a berry so blue,
But they laughed at its dreams, said 'who needs you?'

With a wink and a grin, the flower declared,
'I'm sprouting in spite of all that you've bared!'
The cactus just chuckled, one arm in the air,
Proud of its needles, but still so bare!

In the barren they bloomed, with colors so bold,
Making laughter and joy worth their weight in gold.
So if you're feeling dry, take a note from the blooms,
Even the sparse can bring laughter and rooms.

Echoes in the Garden

In the garden where gnomes love to play,
A carrot said, 'I'm feeling quite gay!'
It swayed to the rhythm, a jig and a hop,
While the radishes giggled, they just couldn't stop.

The onions cried 'foul!' with tears in their eyes,
'Leave us out of your frolics and lies!'
But the carrot kept dancing, and soon in a spin,
Shouted, 'Come join me, let the fun begin!'

A berry bounced in like a ballerina,
Twisting and turning, a real life divina.
'Hold on to your hats, it's a wild ride!
Join the fiesta, let's sweep those tears aside!'

So, in echoes of laughter, the garden rang loud,
With whispering leaves forming a colorful crowd.
Remember, dear friends, even veggies have style,
In the echoes of laughter, life's all about the smile.

The Veil of the Verdant

In the deep of the thicket, where mischief does bloom,
A snail peered out from his leafy green room.
He whispered to friends hidden well in the shade,
'What's better than lettuce? A joke that won't fade!'

A frog with a crown, quite full of himself,
Said, 'I'm royal, but give me no shelf!'
He laughed as he jumped in a puddle of cream,
While the worms in the soil plotted their dream.

Through the veil of the verdant, the whispers did flow,
Of flowered ambitions and how they would grow.
But the wise old oak shrugged, 'Oh, let them play,'
While he napped on the grass, dreaming his day away.

So if you find joy in the bustle of leaves,
Remember the secrets that laughter weaves.
In the cloak of the garden, the fun never ends,
Just join in the folly, where nature pretends.

Thicket Tales Under Moonlight

Under the moonlight, the shadows took flight,
A raccoon in boots danced with glee, what a sight!
He twirled with a twig, wearing leaves on his head,
Singing songs of the night while the sleepy bugs fled.

A beetle with swagger rolled up with a grin,
Said, 'Join me, dear pals, as the mischief begins!'
With the toads on the logs playing drums made of bark,
They partied till dawn, lighting up the dark.

A hedgehog in glasses recited some rhymes,
While fireflies twinkled in sync with the chimes.
The thicket erupted with giggles and glee,
As a fox in a tutu danced by a tree.

So, if you wander where wild things reside,
Under the moon, let your silliness glide.
For in thicket tales, laughter roams free,
Where critters and antics make a fine jamboree.

The Forgotten Flora

In the corner, plants dance with flair,
Pot-bound giggles float through the air.
A cactus claims, 'I'm quite the spiny show!',
While ferns chat secrets that only they know.

With watering cans, we stir that chatter,
'Don't drown us now!' they beg with laughter.
What tales they weave when the lights go dim,
Leaks and drips, just on a whim.

Oh, the timid succulents, shy but sly,
Whispering jokes as the flies pass by.
'It's a jungle out there!' one boldly adores,
While another just giggles and drops its spore.

In this wild fiesta, pots play their part,
Filling the room with their green, quirky heart.
So here's to the greens, in life's vibrant jive,
They charm and tickle, keeping us alive!

Hues of Hydration

In a sunny nook, the colors collide,
A violet cube with nowhere to hide.
'Did you hear the rose?' a cactus did quip,
'It claims it's a queen, I prefer a good slip!'

The aqua droplets, radiant gems,
Run races down leaves like tiny little stems.
'Catch me if you can!' chuckles the thyme,
While mint rolls on laughing, two leaves over time.

The saviors of thirst in cowboy hats bold,
Sipping from puddles, or so I am told.
'Water's for wimps!' laughs a cheeky sprout,
'In this dry land, we simply hang out!'

Each color's a story, each shade brings a jest,
Tales of resilience, a genuine quest.
They sway and they giggle, a garden parade,
Of hues and oddities, perfectly made.

Verdant Vignettes of Survival

A leafy tale unfolds with each sprout,
‘How to thrive when the rains don’t come out!’
Photosynthesis winks in the light,
‘Who needs a spa day? I’m feeling just bright!’

In battles of drought, they gather and scheme,
‘Water balloons’ are a hilarious dream.
Shamelessly mocking the neighbors next door,
Who fuss and fret, while they’re on the floor.

'Bet you can’t eat just one leaf!' they tease,
Pretending to munch, with giddy unease.
With roots intertwined, they throw a big bash,
While the garden gnomes tiptoe with panache.

Each whispering leaf knows how to spread cheer,
Chortling together, oh listen, my dear!
In whispers of green, they throw a grand fight,
It’s a jungle of laughter that lives day and night!

Portraits of Perseverance

In the gallery of greens, a funny display,
Cacti pose proud, with points on their way.
A portrait of patience and watering woes,
'Is that a new friend, or just garden prose?'

There's a jade who knows how to hold its ground,
'When life gives you sun, you dance all around!'
Marigolds giggle, their petals like curls,
'Snap a photo - we're these bright little pearls!'

A bonsai sits looking perfectly prim,
'Hey, I wasn't always this fabulously slim!'
Nature's art speaks in laughter and leaves,
Crafting a canvas that always deceives.

And in the end, as the sunsets unfold,
These leafy crusaders have stories retold.
With joy in their roots, and humor to boot,
They twirl in the breeze, oh how they salute!

The Tenderness of Toughness

In armor made of prickly grace,
These plants have mastered the tough embrace.
They drink from puddles, not from streams,
And laugh in sunlight, or so it seems.

With roots that grip like a best friend’s hug,
They wiggle and squirm, but never a shrug.
They wait for rain, just a tiny sip,
And whisper jokes on a waterless trip.

Leaves that dance in the blazing sun,
Telling each other, 'It’s all in good fun!'
A party in pots, small joys untold,
Each unwatered spike, a story bold.

So here’s to these wonders, quite absurd,
With humor hidden, they rarely are heard.
In the world of plants, they're the sassy crew,
Guardians of secrets, with laughter anew.

Mirage of the Green Souls

In a land where cacti wear party hats,
And leafy greens dance with sassy chats.
They twirl in the breeze, no room for fear,
While making sure to drink just a beer.

Oh, those shiny spines, they tell a tale,
Of desert dreams and a plot to prevail.
When water is scarce, they puff out their chests,
And whisper, ‘Survival, it’s really just quests!’

Amidst the heat, they play hide and seek,
Riddles of moisture, so tricky and sleek.
Their laughter echoes in the dry, dry air,
As they sip the sun with a cheeky flair.

A waltz on the rocks, with shadows that play,
Mirage of delight, in a quirky ballet.
With roots deep and dreams reaching the moon,
They’ll serve up the charm, and then hum a tune.

Buried Treasures of the Sun

Deep underground, where secrets do hide,
These jolly roots have nothing to bide.
They flourish with sunshine like kids in the park,
Unveiling their treasures, both golden and stark.

A dance of old leaves, crispy yet spry,
Whispering tales to the big blue sky.
Each sunbeam a joke, laid out in the sand,
While waiting for the rain with a goofy hand.

Daydreaming while soaking in sun's warm glow,
Letting the world know they're the stars of the show.
With buried connections, their roots intertwine,
A comedy act, in nature's design.

So grab a shovel, come dig for a smile,
Among these rich treasures, let laughter compile.
For every forgotten, drought-sipping shard,
Hides a punchline or two; doesn't life seem hard?

Chronicles of Cracked Earth

In a land of cracks, where the sunlight fries,
The plants hold no grudges, just laughter that flies.
They wiggle and squirm, in the heat of the glow,
Sharing anecdotes of how fast they can grow.

Each fissure a story, each shadow a prank,
Whispered between dandelions and dank.
Raising a toast to the dirt that's so dry,
'We'll thumb our green noses at clouds in the sky!'

With roots that tell tales of endurance and sass,
These little green warriors let nothing surpass.
The dirt may be cracked, but their humor is wide,
Making every hardship a hilarious ride.

So gather round, under the sun's mighty glare,
And listen to plants as they joyfully share.
Although life can crack, they find joy in the spurt,
In the chronicles written by a tough little dirt.

www.ingramcontent.com/pod-product-compliance
Lightning Source LLC
Chambersburg PA
CBHW070322120526
44590CB00017B/2779
* 9 7 8 1 8 0 5 8 1 4 3 1 3 *